First published in 2024 in Great Britain by Esther Y. Xie.

ISBN: 9798321947357

The right of Esther Y. Xie to be identified as the author and illustrator. Canva is acknowledged for the elements in the design.

This book is a gift for every Primary 1 to 5 child in Australia, the United Kingdom, and China.

Cosy up and read it together with your family, then chat about it with your classmates at school.

Visit your local library with your friends and/or family to borrow books for free and discover your new favorite authors and stories.

This Book Belongs TO:

_____

Evelyn Goes to the Party

Evelyn lived in Perth, Australia, with her mum, dad, big brother, and a dog Cameral. It was all good until one day something happened . . .

One scorching sunny day, Evelyn was sleeping in her bedroom, snoring loudly. Suddenly, her alarm went off. She groggily put on her clothes, and brushed her teeth, and then headed to the kitchen for her breakfast.

While she was having her breakfast, the door bell rang.

Evelyn looked out and saw
her friend Harris.
Harris invited her to attend
his birthday party tonight.

Evelyn accepted Harris' invitation, and she happily walked back to her dining table and continued to enjoy her breakfast.

After breakfast, Evelyn told her mum and dad that she is going to Harris' birthday party.

Afterwards, she walked back to her bedroom to prepare partywear using scrap fabric. However, it did not turn out as well as planned.

Fortunately, Evelyn found a perfect present to give to Harris. It was a fascinating toy racing car set that was once her older brother's, and she knew that Harris would love it!

Evelyn placed it on her desk and planned to get it wrapped later because her mother was calling her for her favourite lunch — steamed rice and yellow curry!

Yummy! Steamed rice and yellow curry!"

After enjoying her scrumptious lunch, she asked her father to go shopping with her for partywear for Harris' birthday celebration.

However, her dad said that he needs to finish something urgent and would go with her later.

After her dad finished his work, they were ready to go shopping. As they were driving to their local shop, Evelyn felt very happy.

She imagined herself skipping through the clothing aisles, selecting the best outfits that she wanted to wear.

However, to Evelyn's disappointment, the only shop in the town was closed due to unexpected reasons, and there was no nearby shops. Therefore, Evelyn and her dad had to drive home with empty hands.

After arriving home, she settled into her own bedroom, but nothing seemed right.

One shirt was animal-like for a party, and the other one was boring and plain.

Even without success of partywear, Evelyn decided to move forward. She walked back to her bedroom to wrap up the awesome racing set for Harris' birthday party.

Unexpectedly, her dog Cameral already tore the racing sets into bits before Evelyn could even say STOP!

Evelyn desperately tried
to fix it with duct tape but
it did not work.

Now Evelyn had no partywear, no present and worst of all, not many chances of going to the party.

Then, just as Evelyn was feeling at her lowest, the most wonderful thing occurred—her mum appeared at the door!

No, that wasn't the good part.
It was what Evelyn's mum
held in her hands!

Partywear, a fantastic brand new racing set, and best of all, a big hug from Evelyn's mum's arms.
Her mum told Evelyn that she had secretly kept partywear and a present just in case of an emergency like today.

Mom is my hero, and you are the best.

The End

I hope you have
enjoyed this book.

Acknowledgements

Esther would lke to thank her dad
for paying the fees for the
illustration and helping with some
bits of the story.

Esther would also like to thank her
mom and her brother (Enoch) for
encouraging her while she was
writing the book.

About The Author:

Esther is a nine-year-old girl who loves chewing bubblegum.

She lives in Perth, Australia but she was visiting Scotland with her family when she wrote this book.

Her hobbies are drawing and reading.

Printed in Great Britain
by Amazon

41010585R00021